THE FIREFIGHTER'S COOKBOOK

THE
FIREFIGHTER'S
COOKBOOK

JOHN SINENO

**ILLUSTRATIONS BY
ROBERT PAUL SCUDELLARI**

VINTAGE BOOKS
A DIVISION OF RANDOM HOUSE
NEW YORK

A VINTAGE ORIGINAL,
FIRST EDITION August 1986

9876543

Library of Congress Cataloging-in-Publication Data
The Firefighter's cookbook.
    1. Cookery.   2. Firefighters—New York (N.Y.)
I. Sineno, John
TX652.F486   1986   641.5   85-40862
ISBN 0-394-74429-2

Manufactured in the United States of America

Illustrations by Robert Paul Scudellari

Designed by Naomi Osnos

ACKNOWLEDGMENTS

Since I'm a firefighter with a love of cooking it's natural I'd feel more comfortable in a firehouse kitchen than perched in front of a typewriter. Nevertheless, I find it necessary to acknowledge, with a deep sense of gratitude, those persons who helped make this volume possible.

There's Phil Donahue who granted me national television exposure on his excellent television program and his lovely producer Gail Steinberg. Without these people Random House would hardly be aware of my existence.

There's my Vintage editor Rosann Ward-Dawson, a lady of infinite patience, who tolerated my numerous eccentricities.

There's Lieutenant Harry J. Ahearn, the author of *Ghetto Firefighter*. The lieutenant and I were fellow firefighters assigned to Harlem's Engine Company 58. This man patiently assisted me in placing one word after the other.

There's my good friend Bob Smith, a volunteer firefighter and a director of the New York Firefighter's Burn Center Foundation, whose encouragement and assistance helped me to get this book published.

And there are the selfless firehouse chefs and department personnel who generously contributed many fine recipes; there's my ever-understanding wife Pauline and last, but certainly not least, there's Grandma Sineno whose Neapolitan love of cooking inspired most of my menus.

CONTENTS

INTRODUCTION

When I was appointed to the New York City Fire Department in 1962 and assigned to its probationary school, I had no particular concern regarding firehouse locations, hazardous or otherwise. It was my wife who paced the floor concerned about risks associated with certain parts of New York City. She was amazed at my cavalier attitude; and so was I once I found out that I'd been assigned to the "Fire Factory."

The Fire Factory stands at 114th Street and Fifth Avenue in the heart of the Harlem ghetto, and houses the apparatus of Engine 58 and Ladder 26. At the time of my transfer to that busy engine unit, it was, and remained for many years, the busiest fire company on the face of the earth. And since these units were so busy— and since practice does make perfect—this particular firehouse has had some of the finest professional firefighters ever gathered under one roof. And some of the hungriest.

As my class scattered to the four winds to take up various assignments throughout the metropolitan area, there were those who shared my wife's concern. Now, all these years later, if given a choice of assignments, the Fire Factory and its ever-ravenous crew would be my selection.

After thousands of runs made and fires fought, countless meals prepared—some good, some ordinary, a few sensational—the Fire

Factory is still my home away from home. It is most certainly the place where I perform the role that gives me my greatest satisfaction, my ability to serve as a competent professional firefighter while meeting the culinary demands of an always-hungry group of muscular, loud, raucous, and often profane group of characters.

Walking into a firehouse for the first time is a rather strange experience, or at least it was for me. I was concerned about starting off on the right foot. What would be expected of me? Would I be capable of the job? But the only question the then Captain of Ladder 26, Raymond Kelly, asked me was, "Can you cook?"

Captain Kelly, a man of deep religious convictions, believed his prayers begging for deliverance from what passed for food in his platoon, had finally been answered when I said yes. Later he told me of some of the outrages perpetrated on him and his crew in the name of cooking; and they were *outrages*.

Once one of the men decided to prepare a meal using ordinary rice as the main ingredient; he placed five pounds of rice in a rather smallish pot. It resulted in seven men racing from the kitchen screaming, "It's alive! It's alive!" as the contents bubbled out, over the stove and onto the floor, in seeming pursuit of everything human that crossed its path.

Further, a certain lieutenant who thought he had figured out Burger King's secret hamburger recipe, put hamburger patties—in their buns—in the oven to cook. Unfortunately, he forgot to turn the oven off when the unit responded to an alarm, resulting in a situation far smokier than the inferno outside the firehouse.

On yet another occasion an attempt at spaghetti and meatballs resulted in a debate as to just how long it takes to prepare the pasta. The *alleged* cook finally determined that an occasional toss of a strand of spaghetti at the kitchen ceiling would be the determining factor; when a strand stuck to the ceiling the spaghetti would be ready. Ready at least in the mind of a man who just failed to establish tenure as the company chef.

Despite the great joy I get from cooking good meals for my co-firefighters, I feel compelled to say something about how department chefs are generally treated. It's been said by some that a topnotch firehouse cook must be harrassed during the preparation of a meal. I beg to differ. Those smart aleck comments regarding odors emanating from the kitchen, and their purported similarity to unpleasant aromas wafting from stable areas, are unappreciated and uncalled for. Constant harrassment concerning the length of time spent preparing the meal are as unwelcome as continued criticism regarding rising costs of ingredients. (And since each firefighter must pay for his or her own meals, cost is always a factor.) Nor is it necessary to refer to anything remotely resembling meatloaf as Kennel Ration. Tuna fish casseroles and constant criticism from those non-Italian elements assigned to the firehouses concerning the use of garlic are also unappreciated. Garlic is good for you and if you have any doubts regarding this you may consult my grandmother.

Grandma is an ancient lady of immense proportions who takes credit for a large number of the menus enclosed in this cookbook. Since I'm a modest five foot, eight inches, there are many times when I'd really love to be built like her. It would be nice to look some six-foot-five-inch behemoth in the eye and say, "Sit down, shut up, and eat!"

Grandma would say "Mangia, mangia!" and that's what I say to you. Eat and enjoy. And if it doesn't come out right the first time around, get a friend to harass you during your second effort; who knows, perhaps the guys in the firehouse are right. Riding the chef might just be that extra ingredient needed for a superlative meal. It's worth a shot! After all, nothing ventured, nothing gained. Eat hearty!

John Sineno

A SPECIAL ASSOCIATION: THE NEW YORK FIREFIGHTERS BURN CENTER FOUNDATION

One day while on duty I received a call on the department telephone from a man who introduced himself as Robert Hine, president of the Harvard Business Club. He said he had received permission from the Fire Commissioner to have some of his club members visit Engine 58. He also said he'd heard that I was a pretty good cook and asked if I might prepare a meal for his group when they came to visit. "Sure," I said, "why not?"

Actually, I thought the call was from one of those firehouse jokesters who constantly play practical jokes on the unwary. The supposed "Mr. Hine" then said he'd visit with his group on the following Thursday. "Good, I'll see you then," I said, thinking all the while that I handled this gagster quite well.

Then it suddenly dawned on me, "What if this guy's for real?" To be on the safe side I went upstairs to the officers' room and asked if they had heard about a visit supposedly set up by the Commissioner's office. Both lieutenants said they had heard nothing about any visit from a Mr. Hine or anyone else. "So," I thought, "it's all a gag."

The following Thursday, at about 5:45 P.M., Engine 58 returned to quarters from a run. As the rig headed up the street I noticed a distinguished looking man standing in front of the firehouse. As I dismounted the pumper the man walked up to me, extended his hand and said, "Hi, I'm Robert Hine; my group will be here shortly." His group turned out to consist of eighty men and women. If you think firefighters are fast when they respond to an alarm, you should have seen us doing the shopping, preparing, and cooking in time to feed our illustrious visitors.

It all turned out quite well, everyone having an enjoyable meal and evening. As he was leaving, Mr. Hine asked if there was anything he could do for the firefighters to show his appreciation. I told him I and two other firefighters, Jack Meara and Joe Hickey, were trying to establish a Burn Center in New York City. We felt that too many fire victims were succumbing to their injuries and that a really first-class Burn Center could significantly reduce fatalities. Mr. Hine asked me to arrange a meeting of all concerned so he could be of any assistance in the project.

A week later, steadfast in his promise of help, Robert Hine and his brother Ed, a corporation lawyer, joined firefighters Joe Hickey, Jack Meara, and myself at the quarters of Engine Co. 58, in the first of a series of meetings that resulted in the formation and incorporation of The New York Firefighters Burn Center Foundation.

At about this time New York Hospital-Cornell Medical Center was in the process of trying to establish a Burn Center and asked the New York Firefighters Burn Center Foundation to support its efforts. A meeting was arranged in the Co-Op City Firehouse, Ladder Co. 61, with Dr. David Thompson and Dr. Thomas Shires attending as representatives of New York Hospital. An agreement was reached—of course over a few bowls of rice pudding and some cheesecake—that a joint effort would be made to convince the Health and Hospital Corporation of the dire need for a Burn Center in the metropolitan area.

We know that as a result of this series of events one of the foremost Burn Centers in the world was successfully established in New York Hospital. Firefighters refer to it as "The Miracle on 68th Street." There is a bone of contention, however, as to what factors contributed most to the successful realization of the Burn Center.

Some believe it was the millions of dollars and the expertise provided by New York Hospital; others say it was the eleven thousand signatures that the firefighters presented to the Health and Hospital Corporation. Doubtless, however, it was the rice pudding and cheesecake that served as catalyst in bringing the Burn Center miracle to fruition.

Recognizing the trauma associated with massive burns, the New York Firefighters Burn Center Foundation, an organization of professional and volunteer firefighters, have banded together to help make possible adequate medical care for the most neglected of the hospitalized—the victim of massive burns.

Aware that persons receiving third-degree burns in excess of 25 percent of their anatomy are for all practical purposes dead unless transported to a burn center—*not just any hospital,* but vitally and necessarily a *burn center*—these men whose lives are so closely entwined with such victims have devoted their time, their energy, and no inconsiderable amount of their own funds toward the establishment and maintenance of The Burn Center at the New York Hospital-Cornell Medical Center at Sixty-Eighth Street and York Avenue in New York City.

This ultramodern unit—open to all, regardless of race, creed or economic circumstance—is under the direction of, and staffed by, a team of eminent, full-time, nationally recognized burn treatment experts.

For information, contact The New York Firefighters Burn Center Foundation, % Ladder 61.21 Asch Loop, Bronx, N.Y. 10475.

MAIN COURSES

SWORDFISH KABOBS

Servings: 6

2½ lbs. fresh swordfish
1½ cups oil
½ cup white vinegar
¼ cup sauterne
1 garlic clove, chopped
1 tsp. chopped shallots
2 tbsps. dill weed
1½ tsp. salt
¼ tsp. Tabasco
12 pearl onions
12 mushrooms
4 medium green peppers, sliced (¾″ strips)
4 cherry tomatoes
White rice

Slice swordfish into 1-inch cubes. In a blender combine the oil, vinegar, sauterne, garlic, shallots, dill weed, salt, and Tabasco. Blend for 1 minute on high. Pour marinade over swordfish and place in a glass or plastic bowl; cover and refrigerate for 4–7 hours.

Cook pearl onions in boiling water for 8 minutes. Let cool. Arrange swordfish, pearl onions, mushrooms, and peppers on skewers. Pour marinade from swordfish over skewered fish and vegetables. Broil or grill 3–4 inches from heat for 7–10 minutes. Add the cherry tomatoes. Baste kabobs and broil for an additional 2 minutes, or until tomatoes are tender. Remove skewers and serve on a bed of rice. Garnish with lemon wedges and parsley sprigs.

Note: Although preferably broiled, the kabobs can be baked 15 minutes at 400 degrees.

Lt. William A. Hillery
Fire Academy

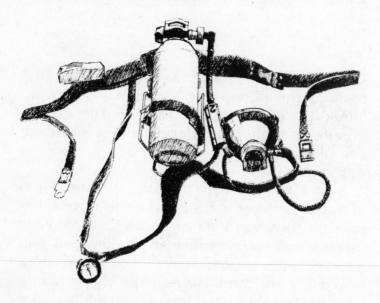

COD FILLET, BARBECUE STYLE

Servings: 2

2 medium onions
2 pieces cod fillet
Salt
Pepper
Paprika
Fresh garlic, sliced thin
Bread crumbs
2 lemons
¼ cup lemon juice
¼ cup water
Parsley

Slice 1 onion and place the slices on a large piece of aluminum foil. Place cod fillet over onions. Sprinkle with salt, pepper, paprika, garlic, and bread crumbs. Chop remaining onion and put over fillet. Squeeze lemon over toppings. Cover with second piece of fillet and repeat above process. Seal aluminum foil tight. Leave one end of foil open and pour in a mixture of lemon juice and water. Seal foil end and place on barbecue rack for 10 to 15 minutes, depending on the thickness of the fish. Garnish with parsley.

John Sineno
Engine 58

POPEYE'S DELIGHT OR PESCE VERDE

Servings: 4

1 lb. fresh spinach, cleaned and rinsed
2 lbs. fresh scrod fillet
1 stick butter or margarine
3 fresh garlic cloves, finely chopped
1 red pepper
½ lb. fresh mushrooms
1 medium onion, chopped
1 large tomato, chopped
⅓ lb. scallops
⅓ lb. medium shrimp, halved
1 fresh lemon
2 ozs. grated Romano cheese

Cover bottom of a large baking dish with spinach. Lay scrod on top of spinach. Set aside. Melt butter in a small frying pan and cook garlic 2 minutes; adding remaining vegetables, scallops, and shrimp. Simmer 5 minutes while stirring in juice of 1 lemon. Pour entire mixture over scrod and spinach. Sprinkle lightly with grated Romano cheese and bake at 350° F for 25 minutes. Serve with fresh French or Italian bread and white wine.

Tom Kennedy
Engine 48

STUFFED FLOUNDER

Servings: 8

1 small onion, diced
2 garlic cloves, diced
3 tbsps. butter
12 ozs. small mushrooms, diced (save caps)
Fresh parsley
Cayenne pepper
Black pepper
8 ozs. bay scallops
8 ozs. crab sticks or sea legs, diced
Juice of 1 lemon
6 ozs. white wine, optional
6 flounder fillets

Sauté onion and garlic in butter. Add mushrooms and parsley and simmer 5 minutes. Add a pinch of cayenne pepper and black pepper. Stir in scallops and crab sticks. Simmer 7 minutes. Add lemon juice. (Wine optional at this point.) Place 3 flounder fillets on a baking tray and lay stuffing over each; top with remaining fillets. Bake 15 minutes in a 350° F oven.

Tom DeLusa
Engine 321

FILLET OF FLOUNDER
WITH SHRIMP STUFFING

Servings: 2

1 lb. fillet of flounder, rinsed
½ lb. shrimp, cleaned
Flavored bread crumbs
Paprika
1 large bell pepper, chopped
1 medium onion, chopped
1 garlic clove, chopped
6 ozs. frozen orange juice
3 ozs. frozen lemonade
2 shakes Worcestershire sauce
Salt and black pepper to taste

Spread oil on bottom of a baking dish. Lay fillet flat. Place shrimp coated with bread crumbs on one end and roll. If shrimp are large they may be boiled for 2 minutes and then rolled into fillet. Arrange in a baking dish and sprinkle with paprika; place in preheated oven at 375° F. Cook until fillet flakes with a touch of a fork, 10–15 minutes, depending on size and thickness of fillet.

Optional Sauce:
Heat oil in a frying pan. Add chopped pepper and cook till tender. Add onion and garlic and cook 3 minutes. Add orange juice and lem-

onade, Worcestershire sauce, salt, and black
pepper. Heat but do not allow mixture to boil.
Pour sauce over cooked fillet and serve.

Tony Catapano
Engine 202

SEAFOOD NEWBURG

Servings: 2

1 cup diced onions
4 tbsps. butter
½ lb. shrimp, cleaned and chopped
½ lb. crab meat
½ tsp. salt, optional
¾ tsp. white pepper
Sherry
½ cup flour
1 cup sour cream
Swiss cheese, grated

Sauté onion in butter till tender; do not brown. Add shrimp and cook till pink. Add crab meat, salt, and pepper. Pour in sherry. Gradually add flour, stirring constantly over very low heat. Simmer 5 minutes. Add sour cream and mix thoroughly. Spoon into a casserole dish and top with Swiss cheese. Cook in a 325° F oven till cheese melts. Bon appetit.

Lt. William Cantley
Engine 16

BAKED BLUE CLAW CRABS

Servings: 6

2 dozen blue claw crabs
1 lb. margarine
1 can tomato sauce, Spanish style
Garlic powder
Onion powder
Parsley
Oregano
½ cup water

Take backs off crabs and clean. Place in a roasting pan. Melt margarine and drizzle over each crab. Pour tomato sauce over each crab. Season with garlic powder, onion powder, parsley, and oregano. Pour water around crabs. Bake in a 400° F oven till crabs are pink in color, 20–30 minutes.

John Sineno
Engine 58

SHRIMP PARMESAN

Servings: 10

5 lbs. large shrimp, cleaned
¾ lb. margarine
8 ozs. mozzarella, grated
1 tbsp. garlic powder
1 tbsp. onion powder
5 ozs. Parmesan cheese, grated
16 ozs. marinara sauce

Place shrimp in a large baking dish. Melt margarine and pour over shrimp. Spread mozzarella evenly over shrimp. Sprinkle with garlic and onion powder and grated Parmesan. Cover with marinara sauce. Cook in a 400° F preheated oven for 15–20 minutes.

John Sineno
Engine 58

SHRIMP CREOLE À LA FAHERTY

Servings: 2

4 tbsps. butter
1 large onion, chopped
1 cup minced green pepper
1 garlic clove, minced
1 tsp. salt
Dash of pepper
¼ tsp. dried rosemary
⅛ tsp. paprika
2 cups stewed tomatoes
1 lb. cooked, shelled and deveined shrimp
2–3 cups hot cooked white rice

Melt butter in a saucepan. Add onion, green pepper, and garlic and sauté 10 minutes. Add salt, pepper, rosemary, paprika, and tomatoes and bring to a boil. Reduce heat and simmer for about 15 minutes. Add shrimp and heat thoroughly. Serve on a bed of fluffy hot rice.

Lt. T. Faherty
Brooklyn/Queens Holy Name Society

BROILED SHRIMP SCAMPI

Servings: 3–4

1½–2 lbs. jumbo or large shrimp, cleaned
12 tbsps. butter or margarine, melted
½ cup chopped parsley
6 garlic cloves, crushed
2 tsps. lemon juice
½ tsp. salt
¼ tsp. pepper
¾ cup oil

Place shrimp on broiler pan. Combine all other ingredients and pour over shrimp. Broil 4 inches from heat for 4 minutes. Turn shrimp and broil for 3 more minutes. Serve.

Note: Some chefs use the broiler pan without the top grill—this allows shrimp to absorb more of the sauce.

Fireman Tom Stack
Brooklyn/Queens Holy Name Society

SHRIMP AND SCALLOPS IN WINE SAUCE

Servings: 12

3 lbs. medium shrimp
3 lbs. bay scallops
4 tbsps. butter
½ cup cornstarch
4–6 cups milk (depending upon desired
      consistency)
1½ cups white wine
6 cups cooked white rice

Cook shrimp and scallops until done. Set aside. Slowly melt butter in a saucepan. Add cornstarch, then milk, stirring constantly. Add wine, shrimp, and scallops. Serve over cooked rice.

Joseph Ginley
Engine 8

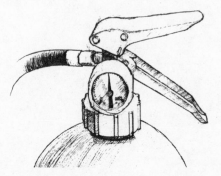

QUICK CHICKEN AND RICE

Servings: 6

1 (3 lb.) chicken, cut into 8 pieces
2 tbsps. oil
1 onion, diced
1 garlic clove, minced
1 large can tomato sauce
Basil, to taste
Oregano, to taste
Salt and pepper
2 cups white rice
4 cups water

Heat oil in a Dutch oven and brown chicken, onion, and garlic. Add tomato sauce, basil, oregano, salt, and pepper. Cook till chicken is tender. In a separate pot, cook rice in water. Pour chicken and sauce over rice. Serve.

John Sineno
Engine 58

Hawaiian Chicken

Servings: 4

2 lbs. boned chicken cutlets
½ cup flour
6 tbsps. oil
2 tbsps. butter
4 garlic cloves, finely chopped
1 large or 2 small onions, cut into ½" strips
3 green bell peppers, cut into 1" chunks
½ cup brown sugar
⅓ cup white vinegar
1 (15 oz.) can pineapple chunks
2 medium tomatoes, cut into eighths
Salt and pepper
Gravy Master

Clean and trim fat from chicken cutlets. Cut in half length-wise, creating 2 separate breasts. Cut breasts into pieces about 1½-inches square. Coat pieces thoroughly with flour and brown in 3 tablespoons oil in frying pan over medium heat until pieces are golden. Drain on paper towels and set aside.

In a 5-quart saucepan, heat remaining oil and butter over medium heat and sauté garlic, onions, and peppers until thoroughly mixed and coated with oil. In a separate bowl combine brown sugar and vinegar. Mix and add to garlic, onion, and pepper mixture. Add undrained pineapple chunks and chicken pieces to vegetable mixture and stir. Simmer, covered, over low heat about 25 minutes, stirring occasionally. Add tomatoes, salt and pepper to taste, and stir. Cover and let simmer another 5 minutes. If necessary, add flour to thicken. Stir in Gravy Master to darken mixture to desired color. Cover, remove from heat, and let stand for 5 minutes. Serve either separately or over rice.

Paul E. Auletta
Ladder 103

CHICKEN MARSALA

Servings: 4

2 lbs. chicken cutlets, pounded
½ lb. butter
¼ cup olive oil
Flour
Salt and pepper, to taste
1 lb. mushrooms
1 shallot
1½ cups sweet Marsala wine
1 bunch parsley, minced
2 lemons, halved

Clean chicken cutlets, removing excess fat. Cut into medallion-size pieces. Melt ¼ pound butter in a skillet and add olive oil. Dredge chicken in flour seasoned with salt and pepper. Shake off excess and sauté to golden brown. Place chicken in an ovenproof pan and set aside. Separate mushroom caps from stems. Mince shallot and mushroom stems, quarter or slice mushroom caps. Melt remaining butter and sauté shallots and mushrooms, and cook until mushrooms release their juice. Remove from heat and add wine and 1 tablespoon minced parsley. Season to taste and simmer for 5 minutes. While mixture is simmering, squeeze juice of 2 lemons over chicken. Pour sauce mixture over chicken, cover, and cook at 350° F for 15–

20 minutes. Garnish with parsley. Serve with noodles alfredo.

Jim Sherwood
Ladder 19

The probie, or rookie, usually gets to go to the store to purchase the ingredients for the company's meals. It's the same in all jobs, the low man on the totem pole gets to do everything everyone else wants to avoid. Anyway, one afternoon I sent a probie to the store with a list of things I needed for the meal. One was a bottle of white wine to be used to baste the roast chicken.

When the probie returned from the store with his arms full of groceries, I noted that he bought red wine instead of white.

"What the hell, I'll use the red," I said.

When I removed the chicken from the oven and set it on the table, all the guys did a doubletake. The roast chicken was PURPLE. It got a good laugh, but I noticed that the color of the chicken didn't diminish anyone's appetite.

From then on I'd occasionally hear someone call out to me as I reported to work, "Hey, Mama, how about making purple chicken tonight?"

CHICKEN OR VEAL IN WINE SAUCE

Servings: 8

4 lbs. chicken or veal cutlets, cut in pieces
¾ cup flour
1 tsp. salt
1 tsp. pepper
1 stick plus 3 tbsps. butter or margarine
1 cup Madeira wine
1 chicken bouillon cube, dissolved
    in ½ cup water
½ tsp. chopped garlic
1 lb. fresh mushrooms, sliced
1 tbsp. lemon juice

Dip meat in flour, salt and pepper. Melt 1 stick butter and brown meat 2–3 minutes on each side. Arrange in a baking dish. Drain fat from skillet. Add wine, bouillon, and garlic and cook over medium heat. When liquid is fully blended, pour over meat. Brown mushrooms in 3 tablespoons butter and sprinkle with lemon juice. Cover meat with mushrooms. Cover dish with aluminum foil. Bake for 40–50 minutes at 350° F.

Jim Munday
Ladder 156

LOW TIDE CHICKEN

Servings: 12

½ cup pure olive oil
½ garlic clove, chopped
6 lbs. boned chicken cutlets
1½ cups water
4 chicken bouillon cubes
1 tsp. thyme
¼ tsp. salt
Pepper
1 lb. fresh mushrooms, sliced
5 boxes frozen leaf spinach

Heat olive oil in a large saucepan. Sauté garlic in oil. Flour chicken and lightly fry, then place in a roasting pan. Strain oil, saving approximately ¼ cup. Pour oil back into saucepan and add the water, bouillon cubes, thyme, salt, and pepper. Cook on high heat until water has almost boiled away, then add mushrooms. Sauté over a low flame for 10 minutes. In a medium pan, cook spinach as per directions on box, drain, and put over chicken. Pour mushrooms and sauce over chicken. Place chicken in oven at 350° F for 10 minutes and serve over rice.

It will look like low tide on the beach if done correctly.

Howard "The Gup" Hill
Ladder 9

NEW ORLEANS JAMBALAYA

Servings: 8–10

2–3 lbs. chicken, cut up
½ cup olive or vegetable oil
3 cups diced cooked ham
2 garlic cloves, minced
3 small onions, chopped
3 (1 lb.) cans whole peeled tomatoes
2 tsps. salt
¼–½ tsp. Tabasco sauce
1 large bay leaf
3 cups diced celery
1 lb. raw shelled and cleaned shrimp
2 cups uncooked white rice
½ cup chopped parsley

In a 5-quart kettle, brown chicken in oil. Take out and set aside. Brown ham, stir in garlic and onions, and sauté for 5 minutes. Return chicken to kettle. Stir in tomatoes, salt, Tabasco sauce, and bay leaf. Bring to a boil, reduce heat, cover, and simmer for 30 minutes. Stir in celery, shrimps, and white rice, making sure all rice is covered by liquid. Simmer 30 minutes longer, or until chicken and rice are tender. Remove bay leaf and add parsley.

Lt. J. Shea
Brooklyn/Queens Holy Name Society

ITALIAN-STYLE CHICKEN

Servings: 4

1 egg
⅔ cup sour cream
Bread crumbs
Pecorino cheese
2½ lbs. chicken, cut up

Mix egg with sour cream. Mix bread crumbs and Pecorino cheese. Dip chicken parts into egg and sour cream mixture, then roll in bread crumbs. Bake in a lightly oiled baking dish in a 350° F oven for 40–50 minutes.

Dominic A. Genovese
Engine 224

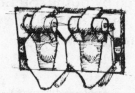

BARBECUED CHICKEN

Servings: 12

4 whole chickens, cut in half
3 cups water
Garlic powder
Onion powder
Paprika
Black pepper
Sugar
1 (44 oz.) bottle ketchup
3 ozs. A-1 sauce
2 ozs. Worcestershire sauce
2 ozs. lemon juice

Place chicken in a pan. Add 2 cups of water. Cook in 400° F oven for about ½ hour. Remove from oven and drain juices from pan. Sprinkle chicken with garlic and onion powder, paprika, and black pepper. Take a handful of sugar and spread generously over chicken. In a large bowl pour ketchup, A-1 sauce, Worcestershire sauce, and lemon juice. Mix well. Pour mixture over chicken. Pour 1 cup water around chicken. Cook in a 400° F oven till top of chicken is crisp, about ½ hour. Remove and serve.

John Sineno
Engine 58

TURKEY CURRY "À LA GIN"

Servings: 12

½ cup finely chopped onion
½ cup finely chopped celery
4 tbsps. margarine
⅓ cup cornstarch
2 cups chicken stock or broth
1 cup tomato juice
½ tsp. Worcestershire sauce
1 tsp. curry powder
Pepper to taste
5 lbs. diced turkey breast
6 cups hot steamed rice

Sauté onion and celery in margarine until tender; add cornstarch and mix thoroughly. Add stock and cook until smooth and thick; add tomato juice, Worcestershire, curry powder, and pepper, then turkey. Heat thoroughly. Pack rice into a greased ring mold and let stand in a warm place 10 minutes. Unmold and fill center with hot curried turkey.

Joe Ginley
Engine 8

TURKEY AU GRATIN

Servings: 12–16

10 lbs. boneless turkey breast
7 lbs. broccoli
1 lb. butter
4 cups flour
2 quarts half-and-half
½ gallon milk
4 lbs. sharp Cheddar cheese, grated
3 tsps. garlic powder
Paprika

Cook turkey 3½ to 4 hours at 350° F. Cool for 15 minutes. Slice thin.

Steam broccoli 4 minutes. Melt butter in a large pot over very low heat. Add flour to melted butter and blend. Cook mixture for 10 minutes, stirring often to prevent burning. Add half-and-half, milk, cheese, and garlic to flour mixture; stir until well blended. Allow to cook until mixture thickens (10–15 minutes), stirring often. Add water if necessary (a thick cheese sauce is desired).

Arrange broccoli spears in a large roasting pan. Drape turkey slices over broccoli. Pour cheese sauce over turkey and broccoli until all is covered. Sprinkle lightly with paprika. Bake for 30–40 minutes at 350° F.

Dave Loper
Ladder 55

FIREHOUSE POT ROAST

Servings: 6

Flour for dredging
Salt and pepper to taste
3½–4 lbs. fresh brisket (1st cut)
3 tbsps. salad oil
⅓ tsp. thyme
½ cup chopped onion
3 garlic cloves, chopped
2 cups canned tomatoes (undrained)
½ tsp. powdered ginger

Mix flour, salt, pepper. Dredge meat in the seasoned flour. Heat the salad oil in a Dutch oven, add the meat, and brown well on all sides. Pour off the fat.

Add the thyme, onion, and garlic. Stir until the onion begins to brown, then add the tomatoes and ginger. Cover tight and simmer until tender (about 2½ hours). Remove to a heated platter. Thicken gravy, if desired, with a little flour mixed with water. Serve with either buttered noodles or mashed potatoes.

Dr. Stanley C. Fell, M.D.
Bureau of Health Services

PEPPER STEAK

Servings: 5–6

6 lbs. skirt steak
8 large bell peppers
2 large onions
1 cup soy sauce
1 cup cream sherry
1 tbsp. garlic powder
1 tbsp. onion powder
Black pepper to taste

Cut skirt steaks into bite-size strips. Put in a roasting pan. Add enough water to fill half of pan. Place in a 400° F oven till meat is brown. Remove and drain off water; set aside.

Cut up peppers and onions and sauté in frying pan till they remain crisp, not soft. Surround meat with peppers and onions. Add soy sauce, cream sherry, garlic and onion powder, and black pepper. Return pan to oven and cook at 400° F till meat is cooked, 20–30 minutes. Serve over a bed of rice.

Captain Pat Buttino
Engine 263

TASTY BEEF ROLLUPS

Servings: 2–3

2 thin slices top round steak, about 8″ diameter
½–¾ lb. sliced baked ham
½ lb. imported Swiss cheese
Flour
Salt and pepper
Grated Parmesan cheese
2 eggs, beaten
Seasoned bread crumbs
Oil

Pound steaks with a meat mallet until very thin. Place 2–3 slices of ham on each steak to cover. Then place 2–3 slices Swiss cheese on top of ham. Take one end of meat and begin to roll up, being careful to keep the ham and cheese in place. Coat each roll with flour, salt and pepper, and grated Parmesan cheese. Dip in egg and then roll each in bread crumbs seasoned with parmesan cheese.

In a large skillet, heat enough oil to cover bottom of pan. Place meat in pan and cook slowly, 20–25 minutes. Turn pieces every few minutes to brown them evenly.

After 25 minutes, cut each roll into 1-inch thick slices and place in a shallow baking dish. Bake in 375° F oven about 10 minutes more.

This will finish cooking all the meat and will melt the cheese. Gravy rendered can be used over rice or noodles.

Capt. Robert Ruszo
Oneonta Fire Dept.

MULLIGAN STEW

Servings: 8

4 lbs. stew beef
Salt and pepper to taste
½ cup flour
⅔ cup cubed carrots
1 cup cubed turnips, uncooked
1 small onion, cut in thin slices
4 cups sliced potatoes

Cut meat into 1½-inch cubes. Sprinkle with salt and pepper and dredge in flour. Grease a frying pan, add meat, and stir constantly to sear all surfaces quickly. When well browned, put in a saucepan. Rinse frying pan with boiling water and pour over meat. Cover meat with boiling water and boil 5 minutes. Reduce heat and simmer until meat is tender (3 hours for lesser cuts).

Add carrots, turnips, onion, salt, and pepper for last hour of cooking. One half hour before stew is done, skim off fat and add potatoes. Thicken with ¼ cup flour mixed with ¼ cup cold water. Cook an additional 5 minutes.

Assistant Commissioner John Mulligan
F.D.N.Y.

IRISH STEW

Servings: 4

1 lb. lamb, cubed
1 lb. beef, cubed
1 medium onion, chopped
2 tbsps. oil
8 cups boiling water
1 large can tomato sauce
5 medium carrots, cut in half
6 medium potatoes, quartered
1 bay leaf
Salt and pepper to taste

Brown lamb, beef, and onions in oil in a large saucepan. Add the boiling water and tomato sauce to meat; simmer 1 hour. Add carrots, potatoes, bay leaf, salt, and pepper; cook until carrots and potatoes are done.

Optional: Add can of corn niblets and/or string beans.

John Sineno
Engine 58

TOM'S CHILI

Servings: 5–6

2½ lbs. chopped meat
1 tsp. adobo (seasoning)
1 can okra
½ tsp. salt
½ tsp. pepper
1½ tsps. chili powder
2 (4 oz.) cans mushrooms, chopped
1 green bell pepper, chopped
1 onion, chopped
1 large can crushed tomatoes
1 large can kidney beans
5 dashes Tabasco
1 (15 oz.) can pinto beans

Brown meat and drain off fat. Put meat in a 1-quart pot and add 2 cups water. Add remaining ingredients. Simmer over low heat for 2 hours. Keep pot covered. Stir occasionally.

Tom Killean
Ladder 55

JIM'S CHILI

Servings: 6–8

1 lb. mild Italian sausage, skinned
  and crumbled
1 lb. ground chuck
1 large yellow onion, diced
2 large garlic cloves, minced
1½ tbsps. chili powder, or to taste
1 (6 oz.) can tomato paste
1½ cups water
1 tbsp. instant coffee
1 tbsp. sugar
1 tbsp. paprika
1 tbsp. oregano
1 tsp. salt
1 tsp. pepper
1 tsp. cumin
1 cup dark red kidney beans, drained
1 cup refried beans

Brown sausage, ground meat, onion, and garlic in a skillet or pot. Add remaining ingredients *except* beans, bring to a boil, cover, and simmer for 1¼ hours. While meat mixture is cooking, combine kidney and refried beans; set aside. After meat is cooked, add beans and stir. Top with grated Monterey Jack cheese and finely chopped green onions.

Capt. James F. McDonnell
Engine 81

VEAL SCALLOPINI OVER NOODLES

Servings: 6

2 cans chicken broth
2 small cans tomato sauce
1½ tbsps. Gravy Master
2 tbsps. basil
2 lbs. veal scallopini
1 lb. mushrooms, sliced
3 garlic cloves
2 tbsps. butter
3 ozs. sherry
Fresh parsley

In a large frying pan, mix broth, tomato sauce, Gravy Master, and basil. Place veal and tomato mixture in a baking dish and cover with foil. Cook for 1 hour in a 375° F oven.

Just before veal is cooked, sauté mushrooms and garlic in butter until golden brown; add sherry and fresh parsley. Pour over veal. If desired, you can thicken sauce with cornstarch. Serve over broad noodles.

Lawrence Cannillo
Engine 82 and Ladder 31

VEAL MARSALA

Servings: 3

1 lb. veal, thinly sliced and pounded
¼ cup grated Parmesan cheese
2 tbsps. flour
Pepper
4 tbsps. butter
1 can sliced mushrooms
1 cup beef broth
2 tbsps. Marsala wine

Cut veal into 2- or 3-inch pieces. Mix cheese, flour, and pepper. Brown veal in butter; add mushrooms and brown. Blend in cheese mixture. Add beef broth and wine. Cover and cook over low heat for 30 minutes, or until meat is tender. Uncover and cook until sauce is desired consistency.

Fireman Jerry Collins
Brooklyn/Queens Holy Name Society

VEAL OR CHICKEN CORDON BLEU

Servings: 12–14

½ lb. boiled ham, sliced
½ lb. Swiss cheese, sliced
12 pieces veal or chicken cutlets, thinly sliced
Flour
Eggs, beaten
Bread crumbs

Cut ham and cheese into strips. Lay cutlets on table. Put a strip of ham and cheese on each cutlet, then roll tight. Add a toothpick to hold together if needed. Use three bowls, one for flour, one for bread crumbs, and one for eggs. Roll meat in flour, then in egg, then in bread crumbs. Put a little oil in a frying pan and fry rolled meat until brown. Place sautéed rolls in a roasting pan and cook in a 400° F oven for about 20 minutes.

John Sineno
Engine 58

PAELLA

Servings: 4

2 tbsps. olive oil
4 links sweet sausage (you can use hot sausage,
   if desired)
1 lb. chicken pieces (legs and thighs)
1 green and 1 red pepper, cored, seeded, and
   cut in small pieces
1 cup finely chopped onion
1 garlic clove, chopped
Saffron, to taste
1 large bay leaf
1 hot dried red pepper, optional
½ tsp. thyme
1 cup canned undrained tomatoes
1 cup uncooked rice
¾ cup water
Salt and pepper to taste
8–12 littleneck clams
8–12 shrimp, peeled and deveined
½ lb. scallops, optional

Heat oil in a skillet. Prick sausages with a
fork and cook about 5 minutes, turning often.
Add chicken pieces, skin side down, and continue cooking until sausages and chicken are
thoroughly cooked, 15–20 minutes. Add pepper,
onion, and garlic to skillet. Stir in saffron, bay
leaf, dried red pepper, and thyme. Add tomatoes, rice, water, salt, and pepper. Cover tightly.

Cook 15 minutes. Add the clams, shrimp, and scallops to rice mixture. Cover again and let cook about 8 minutes more.

Lt. Norman Gordon
Engine 304

POT-POURRI RICHARD

Servings: 8

2 lbs. Italian sausage, cut into bite-size pieces
1 lb. boneless chicken breast, cut into bite-size
    pieces
1 head of broccoli, cut apart
1 head of cauliflower, cut apart
2 lbs. potatoes, cut into bite-size pieces
1 package instant onion soup
1–1½ lbs. London broil
1 small onion, chopped
½ lb. fresh mushrooms, if large, cut in half
1 tbsp. chopped parsley
2 garlic cloves, chopped
3 shakes Worcestershire sauce

Coat a frying pan with oil and heat. Cook sausage, chicken, broccoli, cauliflower, and potatoes, in that order. If necessary, add oil while cooking. When each item is cooked, place in a baking pan. Place baking pan on low heat and add instant onion soup (mix with hot water).

Broil or barbecue the beef while frying other items. When steak is cooked, cut up into strips and place in baking pan. Any juice from steak should be placed in pan.

Sauté onion, mushrooms, parsley, and garlic in frying pan until onion is soft. Add Worcestershire sauce and pour over into baking pan. (If more juice is needed, add hot water to baking pan.)

You may add or use other vegetables of your choice. If you want to make Pot-Pourri Richard Supreme, just add shrimp.

Tony Catapano
Engine 202

SAUSAGE AND CHICKEN MÉLANGE

Servings: 14

½ cup olive oil
7 lbs. medium potatoes, cut in eighths
3 lbs. large green peppers, sliced in eighths
4 medium onions, sliced
2 tbsps. oregano
Salt and pepper to taste
4 broiling chickens, cut up
6 lbs. Italian sausage (sweet or hot, as desired)

Pour olive oil into a roasting pan. Alternate layers of potatoes, peppers, and onions in pan, seasoning with oregano, salt, and pepper. Place chicken parts on top and season as above. Place sausages on top of chicken parts and season as above. (Juice from sausages will seep down through other ingredients.) Place in a 350° F oven and cook for about 1½ hours. Check periodically and turn ingredients.

I did a lot of cooking as a firefighter, less as a lieutenant, and even less as a captain. I cooked the above meal one night as captain of Ladder 119, Williamsburg, Brooklyn. Before we could eat, we responded to a fire alarm in a factory building. Rescue 2 was already at the fire. Naturally, they left before we did. When we finally returned to quarters, we found a note on the kitchen table thanking us for a good meal. It was signed Rescue 2.

Chief Adolph S. Tortorielle
Support Service, Retired

SAUSAGE AND PEPPERS

Servings: 6

6 lbs. Italian sausage
8 bell peppers, cubed
2 large onions, chopped
1 cup soy sauce
1 tbsp. garlic powder
1 tbsp. onion powder
Black pepper

Put sausage in a roasting pan. Add enough water to cover the bottom of the pan. Cook in a 400° F oven for 30 minutes, or until sausage is golden brown. Remove and drain fat. Cook peppers and onions till tender in water. Cut sausages into bite-size pieces and return to pan. Add soy sauce to pan and 1 cup water (from the peppers and onions). Pour drained peppers and onions over sausage and add garlic and onion powder, and black pepper to taste. Return to oven for an additional 15 minutes. Serve.

Captain Pat Buttino and John Sineno
Engine 263 and Engine 58

A POLISH FAREWELL TO LENT

Servings: 14 people or 7 firefighters

5 lbs. fresh kielbasa (not smoked)
5 lbs. sauerkraut

Place kielbasa in a large pot and cover with water. Bring to a boil and simmer for 45 minutes and add sauerkraut. Continue to simmer for 30 minutes. Serve with horseradish or mustard.

James E. Kohler
Deputy Commissioner F.D.N.Y.

POTTED PORK CHOPS

Servings: 2

1 onion, finely chopped
4 pork chops
1 package brown gravy mix
8 ozs. large egg noodles

Brown onions in butter in a 5-quart pot. Add pork chops and brown on both sides. Add 3 cups water and brown gravy mix. Cover and let simmer for 45 minutes to 1 hour until meat is tender. Serve over a bed of noodles.

Fireman Jim Harris
Brooklyn/Queens Holy Name Society

BARBECUED SPARERIBS

Servings: 12

8 pounds spareribs (cut into individual
    portions)
½ lb. margarine
4 onions, chopped or cut into small pieces
2 cups water
8 ozs. ketchup
4 tbsps. vinegar
6 tbsps. Worcestershire sauce
1 tablespoon prepared mustard
1 tsp. pepper

Brown individual servings of ribs in a frying
pan. Pour out fat drippings. Melt margarine in
the same frying pan with spareribs and add onions. Sauté for 2 minutes. Put spareribs and onions in a large baking pan. Mix all other
ingredients and put into the baking pan. Cook
for about 2 minutes, stirring often. Cover pan
with aluminum foil. Place in a 400° F oven and
cook for about 2 hours.

James J. Gregorio
Engine 315

PORK CHOPS IN GERMAN SAUCE

Servings: 8

8 pork chops, about 1″ thick
3 lbs. sauerkraut
2 cups raisins
½ cup honey
2 (6 oz.) cans beer
2 (6 oz.) cans dark beer
1 tsp. sage
1 tsp. tarragon
2 tsps. parsley flakes
¼ tsp. black pepper

Brown pork chops. Add remaining ingredients to pork chops and fat and cook in covered pan for 30 minutes. Serve with applesauce and cinnamon.

Eugene T. Walsh, Jr., Fire-Medic
Engine 54

SWEET AND SOUR SHORT RIBS

Servings: 6

3–3½ lbs. short ribs
⅓ cup plus 2 tbsps. flour
3 tbsps. fat
⅛ tsp. pepper
1½ cups sliced onions
1½ sliced garlic cloves
2 cups hot water
1 bay leaf
½ cup vinegar
4 tbsps. brown sugar
1 cup ketchup
½ tsp. salt
Cooked noodles

Cut short ribs into serving pieces; remove excess fat. Dredge in ⅓ cup flour and place in frying pan. Brown well on all sides in hot fat. Remove to a heavy pot; add pepper, onions, and garlic to fat and cook until tender; add to short ribs. Combine remaining ingredients except the 2 tablespoons flour and noodles and pour over ribs. Cover tight and cook slowly until tender, 2½–3 hours. Remove ribs to a serving plate and keep warm. Pour off fat from gravy; stir in remaining flour and 2 tablespoons of water. Serve on hot buttered noodles.

Deputy Chief William J. Coleman
Chief in Charge, Bureau of Health Services,
F.D.N.Y.

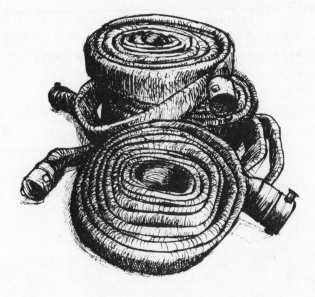

STUFFED FRESH HAM

Servings: 8–12 (depending on size of ham)

1 fresh ham (13–18 lbs.) with a pocket for
    stuffing
4 to 16 links Italian sausage

Put ham into a roasting pan and surround with water. Cook in a 400° F oven for about 2 hours. Remove. Strip sausage from casings and stuff pocket of ham with sausage meat. Add more water to pan if needed. Return to oven till ham is cooked, about 1 hour longer.

When ham is done, drain off juice from pan and put into a can or pot. Place in refrigerator for ½ hour. Remove the fat that has risen to the top. Use juice to make pork gravy.

John Sineno
Engine 58

SAUERBRATEN

Servings: 12–14

5–8 lbs. venison roast
2 tbsps. pickling spices
½ cup sugar
Salt and pepper
1 quart cider vinegar
4 onions, chopped

Place all ingredients in a pot. Cover with 1 inch of water. Refrigerate for 3–4 days. Pour juice out and save. Brown meat and onions. Then pour juice in, 1 cup at a time, and cook till all is evaporated, about 2 hours.

Joe Bryant
Rescue 3

It was late November in 1970. I was just a new probie assigned to L. 26. Traditionally, in the firehouse at that time, the pre-diet era, everyone was in on the meal. I don't know how many vegetarians there were on the job at the time, but I was sure I was the only one. It was still very weird not to eat meat back then. For my first few tours I didn't eat anything, but that didn't work because I was starving. So finally one night I got up the nerve to bring in my own meal and had the audacity to cook it on John

Sineno's stove. I was nervous about everyone ribbing me, so I started cooking early. Then Sineno came in, took one look at what I was cooking, and I waited for the sneers, but they didn't come. John just started asking me, "What's this, what's that, and what the hell are you going to do with all these almonds?"

It was my first meeting with John Sineno, Head Chef, at E. 58 and Lad. 26. Other fellows cooked, but John was the CHEF. He made me feel great that night and we became friends. If ever I was cooking he would always ask me what I was making. Even until this day I wish I could have jumped in on John's aromatic, delicious looking, but unfortunately nonvegetarian meals. John was always calling to me, "Plenty of salad Kenny—do you want any?" John never ceased to amaze me, whether cooking for 10, 20, 30, or 100, he always seemed to be having a good time. His little quips of philosophy, which I called Sinenoisms, were my after-dinner mints. "Chef" John Sineno is definitely one of the legends in firehouse tales.

Kenny Ruane
Ladder 16

KENNY'S VEGETARIAN DISH

Servings: 3

1 onion, sliced
1 green pepper, sliced
¼ head cabbage thinly sliced (core discarded)
1 small broccoli, chopped
1 cup mung bean sprouts
½ cup raw almonds
1 cup brown rice, cooked
Tamari soy sauce

Sauté onion and pepper. Add cabbage and broccoli and sauté till tender. Add bean sprouts and almonds. Toss. Serve over cooked rice with Tamari soy sauce.

Kenny Ruane
Ladder 16

STUFFED GREEN BELL PEPPERS
WITH RED SAUCE

Servings: 12

6–7 cups cooked rice
1 jar olive condite
Garlic powder
Salt and pepper
Sweet basil, to taste
Parsley, to taste
12 green peppers, tops removed and seeded
Oil

Sauce:
1 small onion, chopped
2 garlic cloves, minced
2 cans whole tomatoes
Salt and pepper, to taste
Sweet basil, to taste
Parsley, to taste
Oil

Combine rice, condite, garlic, salt, pepper, basil, and parsley. Parboil peppers and let cool. Fill each one with rice mixture. Heat oil in a frying pan and quickly sauté peppers on all sides. Turn peppers upside down and fry tops, just enough to brown stuffing on top of peppers.

For the sauce, sauté onion and garlic in oil. Core tomatoes and add to pan. Add salt and pepper, sweet basil, and parsley. Simmer 45 minutes. Set aside 30–60 minutes. When sauce is ready, set peppers straight up in a roasting pan. Pour red sauce over peppers. Cook in a 350° F oven for about ½ hour, or until peppers are soft.

John Sineno
Engine 58

Perhaps the saddest occasion I cooked for was Larry Fitzpatrick's funeral.

Larry and I had worked together for years. He then transferred to Rescue 3. He died trying to save one of "the brothers."

Fireman Frisby, Ladder 28, was trapped in a blazing room on an upper story of a Harlem tenement. He was able to reach one of the windows and to call for help.

Fitzpatrick went to the roof of the building. He tied a rope around his waist, fastened the other end to a chimney, and went over the side. He lowered himself to the window where Frisby was waiting. Frisby leaned out the window and grabbed onto Larry. Larry slowly played out the rope as they started down to the alleyway below them.

Then the rope broke.

That night the sad signal 5–5–5–5 announcing the deaths of Firefighters Fitzpatrick and Frisby was transmitted to all City firehouses.

Captain Ryan asked me to do the collation. I had to feed the thousands of firefighters who attended Larry's funeral. The Fitzpatricks had lived in Merrick, a suburb of the City, and the Merrick Volunteer Fire Department graciously offered the use of its firehouse for the meal after the services.

Everyone who turned out that day to honor Larry ate a good meal. I didn't eat much myself —the lump in my throat was just too big. We fed over 4,000 people.

ARTICHOKE PIE

Servings: 6

1 cup diced mozzarella cheese
½ can cut artichokes, diced
½ cup diced pepperoni
¼ cup grated cheese
4 eggs, beaten
1 frozen pie shell

Mix all ingredients. Pour into pie shell and bake 45–50 minutes in a 350° F oven.

Danny Prince
Ladder 156

ITALIAN SPINACH PIE

Servings: 6

1 pastry shell
1½ cups frozen spinach, defrosted
4 tbsps. butter
Salt and ground pepper to taste
½ lb. ricotta cheese
3 eggs, slightly beaten
½ cup grated Parmesan cheese
½ cup heavy cream
1 nutmeg, grated

Cook spinach with butter, salt, and pepper; drain thoroughly. To spinach add ricotta cheese, eggs, Parmesan, cream, and nutmeg to taste. Pour mixture into pastry shell and bake in a moderate oven (375° F) for 30 minutes, or until the crust is brown and cheese mixture set.

Joseph Bruno
First Deputy Fire Commissioner F.D.N.Y.

"FIREMEN DO EAT QUICHE"

Servings: 6

3 cups grated zucchini
1 small onion, chopped
1 cup Bisquick
4 eggs
½ cup vegetable oil
½ cup grated Parmesan cheese
½ tsp. parsley (¼ cup fresh)
½ tsp. marjoram
¼ tsp. salt
¼ tsp. fresh pepper

Mix all ingredients. Bake in a large greased pie plate at 350° F for 30 minutes, or until golden brown.

Eugene T. Walsh, Jr., Fire-Medic
Engine 54

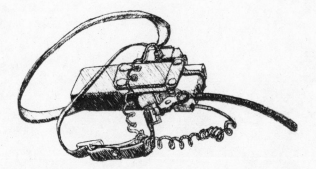

PASTAS AND SOUPS

Plain Marinara Sauce (Basic Sauce)

Servings: 12

2 gallon can crushed tomatoes
Salt
Pepper
Fresh basil, chopped
1 tsp. mint
Bunch of parsley, finely chopped
4 ozs. margarine
½ cup olive oil
7 garlic cloves, chopped
1 onion, chopped
3 carrots, chopped
1 cup dry white wine

Heat crushed tomatoes to boiling. Let simmer and add 1 can of water, salt and pepper to taste, chopped basil, mint, and parsley. Let simmer for 1 hour. Heat margarine and olive oil in a frying pan. Add garlic, onion, and carrots. Let simmer till brown. Add wine; simmer till wine boils. Put mixture through a strainer into tomato sauce. Discard garlic and onion remains. Add carrots to sauce. Add salt and pepper to taste. This basic sauce can be modified for a variety of dishes by adding different spices and meats.

John Sineno
Engine 58

PESTO SAUCE

Servings: 4

¼ lb. fresh basil leaves
2 garlic cloves
2 tbsps. olive oil
2 tbsps. grated Parmesan cheese

Wash basil thoroughly and remove stems. Dry well. Place ingredients in a blender. Blend until well chopped; be sure not to liquefy. Store sauce in a well-sealed jar. Cover sauce with a layer of olive oil. Serve sauce at room temperature on hot cooked spaghetti or linguini. If desired, add cheese or butter to the pesto and macaroni or even a little water to avoid dryness.

Joseph Bruno
First Deputy Fire Commissioner, F.D.N.Y.

WILD IRISH "ROUGE"
A PASTA MÉLANGE

Servings: 3–4

Olive oil
1 lb. spaghetti (preferably thin)
5 strips bacon
1 large garlic clove, crushed
1¼ lbs. margarine or butter
1 (16 oz.) can sauerkraut
1 (4 oz.) can sliced mushrooms
Caraway seeds
Coarse pepper
6 ozs. red pimiento slices
Parmesan cheese, grated
Parsley flakes

Bring 3 quarts water to a boil with a pinch of salt and 4 tablespoons olive oil. Add spaghetti and boil for about 11 minutes.

Meanwhile, fry bacon, chop, and return to frying pan. Add garlic, margarine, 3 tbsps. olive oil, sauerkraut, mushrooms, a pinch each of caraway seed and coarse pepper. Sauté, tossing frequently; do not burn.

Put pimientos and 2 tablespoons oil in a small pot but do not heat until spaghetti is drained and in a warm bowl. Add sauerkraut mixture to spaghetti. Toss. Garnish with 4 tablespoons grated cheese, sprinkle with parsley, and pour heated pimientos over.

Jack "Black Jack" McLaughlin
Battalion Chief, 53rd Battalion

FROM SICILY WITH LOVE

PASTA WITH SARDINES, PALERMO STYLE

Servings: 4

2 cups leaf tops from fennel (if unavailable, use
    1 tablespoon fennel seeds wrapped in
    cheesecloth)
½ cup olive oil
2 tbsps. chopped onion
4 flat anchovy fillets, chopped
⅓ cup pignoli nuts
1 tbsp. raisins, soaked in cold water for 15
    minutes
1½ tbsps. tomato paste
½ package saffron threads, dissolved in 1 cup
    water
Salt and pepper, to taste
3 (3¾ oz.) cans boneless sardines packed in
    olive oil, drained
1 pound bucatini or perciatelli macaroni
    (imported from Italy)
½ cup unflavored bread crumbs, lightly toasted
    in oven

Wash fennel tops in cold water. Bring 4–5
quarts of water to a boil in the pot that you will
use to cook the pasta. Cook the tops for about 10
minutes. Turn off heat and remove the greens;
do not discard the water. Do the same if using

fennel seeds. Gently squeeze the moisture out of the greens and chop.

Choose a pan large enough to contain all the ingredients except the pasta. Put in the olive oil, onion, and anchovies. Heat over a medium flame, stirring occasionally. When the onion becomes translucent, put in the chopped fennel and cook for 5–6 minutes. Add the pignoli, raisins, tomato paste, and dissolved saffron. Add salt and pepper. Cook at medium heat until the water in the pan has bubbled away completely. Put in the sardines, turn them for a few seconds, and then turn off the heat. Cook the pasta al dente. When the pasta is almost cooked begin to heat the sauce over low heat. Place the pasta in a warm bowl, add the sauce and bread crumbs, toss thoroughly, and let the mixture rest a few minutes before serving.

Rev. Guy Vinci
Fire Department Chaplain

BAKED MACARONI

Servings: 12–15

3 lbs. elbow or ziti macaroni
5 cans mushroom soup
8 ozs. sharp cheddar cheese, grated
8 ozs. Parmesan cheese, grated
4 (4 oz.) cans mushrooms (caps and stems),
    drained

Cook macaroni and transfer to a baking dish.
Heat soup adding 1 can of water to each can of
soup. Pour soup, cheeses, and mushrooms into
baking dish and mix well. Cook in a 350° F oven
for 25–30 minutes.

John Sineno
Engine 58

If there's anything firemen love to do more
than fight fires, it's to talk about fire, over a
good meal.

We were in the kitchen swapping fire stories
one night when Jerry O'Keefe asked me if I re-
membered a particular fire we had both been at.

"You remember, John, that job we had up the
street about a year ago?"

"You mean the ravioli fire?" I asked.

"The WHAT fire?" asked Jerry.

"The ravioli fire," I said. "I remember fires by what I cooked that day."

It wasn't long after that that I noticed the men gently pulling my leg by referring to fires from then on as "The London broil fire," "the chicken cordon bleu fire," etc.

If there's anything firemen love to do more than talk about fires, it's to pull my leg, and probably eat it if I cooked it!

MANICOTTI

Servings: 6

Shells:
3 eggs
1 cup sifted flour
1 cup club soda
Pinch of salt

Filling:
½ lb. ricotta cheese
¼ lb. mozzarella cheese, shredded
1 egg
¼ lb. Parmesan cheese, grated
Salt and pepper to taste
Parsley

Beat eggs well with a whisk or fork; gradually add flour, blending thoroughly. Add club soda and salt; continue stirring until batter is smooth. Set in refrigerator for 1 hour before cooking. (Be sure to stir mixture before using.) Heat a small cured crepe pan—6 inches in diameter. Add a couple of tablespoons of batter at a time. Cook on one side only until they are set. Do not brown. Transfer onto wax paper; continue until all batter is used.

Mix all filling ingredients in a bowl. Place 2 tablespoons of filling on each crepe. Roll. Place manicotti on a baking sheet and cover with tomato sauce. Bake in a preheated 350° F oven for 15 minutes, or until manicotti are piping hot throughout.

Danny Prince
Ladder 156

FIRE COMMISSIONER'S FETTUCCINE

Servings: 8

½ lb. butter
½ lb. prosciutto, thinly sliced and shredded
¾ lb. fresh mushrooms, thinly sliced
1½ pints heavy cream
½ cup grated Parmesan cheese
Tomato sauce
Fettuccine noodles

Melt ¼ pound butter in a frying pan. Sauté prosciutto and mushrooms; set aside. Melt remaining ½ pound butter in cream over low flame; gradually add grated cheese, stirring constantly. Cook until well blended and thick. Set aside. Heat tomato sauce. Cook fettuccine; drain and return to pot. Ladle half of the red sauce into fettuccine and mix. Gradually add half the white sauce and stir till fettuccine is well coated. Add remaining red and white sauce. The fettuccine should be well coated and a light orange color. Dish into individual bowls. Sprinkle prosciutto and mushrooms on each dish.

Commissioner Joseph Spinnato, F.D.N.Y.

I once asked "Spooky" Adrian to taste the macaroni to see if it was done. Spooky picked up a strand and I thought he was going to taste it. Instead, he threw the strand up to the ceiling. He said, "If it sticks, it's done."

It stuck.

LINGUINE WITH CLAM SAUCE

Servings: 3–4

2 (7½ oz.) cans whole baby clams, or 2 cups
    fresh minced clams
¼ cup olive oil or salad oil
¼ cup butter or margarine
3 large garlic cloves, minced
2 tbsps. chopped parsley
1½ tsps. salt
8 ozs. linguine
Parmesan cheese, grated

Drain canned clams, reserving ¾ cup of liquid; set aside. Slowly heat oil and butter in a skillet. Add garlic and sauté until golden. Do not let garlic brown. Remove skillet from heat. Stir in clam liquid, chopped parsley, and salt. Bring to a boil, reduce heat, and simmer uncovered for 10 minutes.

While mixture is simmering, boil linguine till al dente (chewy) in 3 quarts water, 1 teaspoon salt, 3 tablespoons olive oil.

Add clams to skillet after mixture has finished simmering. When linguine is cooked, drain and pour in ingredients of skillet and sprinkle with cheese.

Lt. J. Shea
Brooklyn/Queens Holy Name Society

CAVATELLI AND BROCCOLI

Servings: 4

4 garlic cloves, chopped
1 oz. olive oil
1 head broccoli (tough stems removed), chopped
2 cups chicken broth
1 lb. frozen cavatelli
4 tbsps. butter
Salt to taste
Pepper to taste, optional
Grated Parmesan cheese

In a wok or frying pan, sauté chopped garlic in oil. Before it browns, add chopped broccoli and stir-fry until al dente. Add broth to cover broccoli and cook on a low flame until tender. Cook cavatelli till desired doneness. Drain and place on a flat long plate. Place butter on cavatelli and fold in. Pour broccoli over cavatelli, season with salt and pepper, and top with cheese. Serve piping hot.

Capt. Vincent Dipippo
Engine 83

CARMELA'S SPECIAL BEAN SOUP

Servings: 4

⅛ cup of your favorite cooking oil
1 medium onion, diced
2 large garlic cloves, diced
½ pound chopped chuck
3 sausage links (hot or sweet, to taste)
1 can Italian plum tomatoes, strained
3 celery stalks, cut into chunks
Salt and pepper to taste
4 cups water
1 large can cannellini beans
1 cup small elbow macaroni

Heat cooking oil in a 2-quart saucepan. Add onion and garlic and sauté lightly. Remove from oil and set aside. Add chopped meat to pan and brown; remove and set aside. Brown sausage links and remove; cut into bite-size chunks and set aside. Pour strained tomatoes into oil, stirring gently, and let simmer for 10 minutes. Add celery and cook another 5 minutes. Return all cooked ingredients, stirring to let meats absorb sauce. Cook for 1 hour. Add seasoning to taste. Pour in water and add beans; cook for an additional ½ hour. Meanwhile cook elbow macaroni. When soup is done, add cooked macaroni and stir. Serve immediately. Grated Parmesan cheese can be served with soup. Soup can be poured over hard Italian biscuits or over Italian bread.

Carmela Rosseno Ciance
District Office 12

ARIZONA MOUNTAIN SOUP

Servings: 8

1¼ cups dry pinto beans
3 slices bacon, chopped
2 medium onions, finely chopped
2 garlic cloves, minced
1 (16 oz.) can tomatoes, cut up
1½ cups brown rice, cooked
2 tsps. salt
½ tsp. paprika
¼ tsp. pepper

Rinse beans. Combine beans and 3 cups of water in a 5-quart kettle or Dutch oven. Cover, let stand overnight or bring to boiling, reduce heat, and let simmer 2 minutes. Let stand 1 hour. Do not drain. Simmer, covered, for 2 hours, or until beans are tender. Drain, reserving 2 cups of liquid. Cook bacon in Dutch oven until almost crisp. Add onion and garlic. Cook and stir until the vegetables are tender but not brown. Stir in the cooked pinto beans, tomatoes, rice, salt, paprika, and pepper. Add reserved bean liquid and 2 cups of water. Bring mixture to boiling. Cover and simmer 1 hour, stirring occasionally. If soup is too thick, add water.

Don Schwerdt
Engine 4, Springfield, N.J.

CHICKEN RICE SOUP

Servings: 6–8

1 whole chicken, cut up
1 tbsp. chopped parsley
4 large carrots, diced
2 cups rice
2 chicken bouillon cubes
Parmesan cheese to taste

Wash chicken and put in a stockpot. Cover with water (approximately 6 cups) and add parsley and carrots. Bring to a slow boil and cook till chicken is done. When chicken is cooked, remove from pot, bone and shred. In the same pot, add rice and bouillon cubes. Cover and cook until rice is done. Add shredded chicken and serve. Garnish with Parmesan cheese.

John Sineno
Engine 58

CHICKEN AND ESCAROLE SOUP

Servings: 6–8 (depending upon amount of ingredients used)

1 chicken, cut up
1 celery stalk, chopped
4 carrots, chopped
1 onion, chopped
Salt and pepper to taste
2 bunches escarole
1 lb. chopped meat
Garlic
Bread crumbs
Cheese
Parsley

Use amount of ingredients as desired to taste.

Cover chicken with water, cover and bring to a boil. Add celery, carrots, onion, salt, and pepper. Wash and clean escarole. In a separate pot, boil escarole for 20 minutes to ½ hour. Drain and let cool. Season chopped meat with garlic, bread crumbs, cheese, and parsley. Mold seasoned chopped meat into small meatballs, the size of dimes. Remove chicken from soup; bone and shred. Add meatballs, escarole, and shredded chicken to broth. Simmer for an additional 15–20 minutes.

John Sineno
Engine 58

TORTELLINI MEATBALL SOUP

Servings: 16–20

2 gallons water
6 beef bouillon cubes
6 chicken bouillon cubes
1 package soup greens, finely chopped
Pepper to taste
Garlic powder, to taste
2 lbs. ground beef
1 large head escarole, cleaned and chopped
2 packages fresh spinach, cleaned and chopped
2 lbs. tortellini
1 egg, beaten
2 tbsps. chopped fresh parsley
2 tbsps. Worcestershire sauce

Into a large soup pot, put water, beef and chicken bouillon cubes, soup greens, pepper, and garlic powder. Simmer for 1 hour. Form beef into meatballs.

After soup has simmered for 1 hour, add meatballs, escarole, spinach, and tortellini. Simmer till meatballs are thoroughly cooked. Add egg and parsley. Five minutes before serving, add Worcestershire sauce.

Capt. Pat Buttino
Engine 263

VEGETABLE SOUP EXPRESS
"A 6-MAN FIREHOUSE DELIGHT"

Servings: 6 hungry firemen

3 tbsps. butter
6 medium onions, chopped
6 celery stalks, chopped
3 sprigs parsley, finely chopped
1 bay leaf
8 large tomatoes, puréed
8 carrots, diced
1 lb. string beans, diced
6 medium potatoes, cut into large cubes
8 beef bouillon cubes
⅛ tsp. ground pepper
Salt to taste

In a 10-quart pot, sauté in butter the onions, celery, parsley, and bay leaf. Add water as needed in ¼ cup amounts for 20 minutes. In a 5-quart pot, add tomatoes, carrots, string beans, potatoes, and 2 quarts cold water. Cook over a medium flame for 15 minutes, then over a low flame for an additional 5 minutes. Pour vegetable mixture into 10-quart pot. Add another quart water and bouillon cubes. Bring to a low boil with lid for 30 minutes. Add the pepper and salt to taste.

J. d'Emic
Engine 248

POTATO SOUP

Servings: 12

3 lbs. beef soup bones, cracked
3 medium potatoes, peeled and cut in large
    pieces
4 medium carrots, scraped and cut in large
    pieces
2 medium turnips, peeled and coarsely chopped
2 medium onions, cut in quarters
⅓ cup snipped parsley
3 tbsps. butter
3 quarts water
4 tsps. salt
1 cup half-and-half
2 egg yolks, beaten
Grated Parmesan cheese
Snipped parsley

Place soup bones in a large baking pan. Bake in a preheated 450° F oven 15–20 minutes, or until browned. In a large kettle, sauté potatoes, carrots, turnips, onions, and ⅓ cup snipped parsley in butter until slightly browned. Add water, salt, and browned soup bones. Cover, and simmer over low heat for about 1 hour.

Remove any meat from bones, and discard bones. Strain soup, reserving stock and vegetables. Place vegetables in a blender and purée, or force through a fine sieve. Mix together stock, pieces of meat, and puréed vegetables. Bring to a boil and gently boil until soup reaches 2½ quarts. Before serving, heat soup. Combine half-and-half, and beaten egg yolks. Stir a small amount of soup into the egg mixture, and return to soup. Heat until slightly thick. Serve with a sprinkle of Parmesan cheese and snipped parsley.

Don Schwerdt
Engine 4, Springfield, N.J.

NEW YORK CLAM CHOWDER

Servings: 6

¼ lb. bacon, chopped
1 onion, chopped
1 (16 oz.) can whole tomatoes
½ tsp. salt
¼ tsp. pepper
1 carrot, sliced
1 cup cubed potatoes
2 cups hot water
1 dozen large clams, chopped, with their juice
    (must be hard clams)
1 tsp. thyme

Brown bacon with onion. When onion is soft, add tomatoes, salt, pepper, carrots, potatoes, and water. Boil until potatoes and carrots are done. Add clams, thyme, and clam juice. Simmer for 5 minutes.

Fireman Tom Stack
Brooklyn/Queens Holy Name Society

Manhattan Fish Chowder

Servings: 6

1 lb. fish fillets
¼ cup chopped bacon or salt pork
½ cup chopped onion
2 cups boiling water
1 (1 lb.) can whole tomatoes
1 cup diced potatoes
½ cup diced carrots
½ cup chopped celery
¼ cup ketchup
1 tbsp. Worcestershire sauce
1 tsp. salt
¼ tsp. thyme

Cut fish into 1″ pieces. Fry bacon until crisp. Add onion and cook until tender. Add water, tomatoes, potatoes, carrots, celery, ketchup, and seasonings. Cover and simmer 45 minutes until the vegetables are tender. Add fish. Cover and simmer about 10 minutes, until fish flakes easily with a fork. Sprinkle with parsley and serve.

Don Schwerdt
Engine 4, Springfield, N.J.

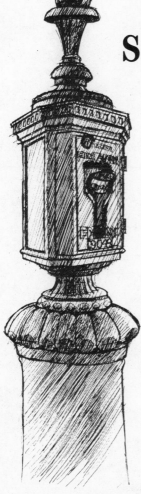

 SIDE DISHES

BAKED MUSSELS

Fresh mussels, amount desired
¼–½ cup water
Flavored bread crumbs
Margarine, melted
Marinara sauce

Put mussels in a frying pan with water and steam open. Once opened, drain off water. Remove one part of the shell and discard. Place mussels in shells in a baking pan and top with bread crumbs. Drizzle with margarine. Pour marinara sauce over mussels and place in a 375° F oven for 10–15 mins. Serve immediately.

John Sineno
Engine 58

BAKED CLAMS BELLISSIMO

Servings: 12

3 tbsps. oil for frying
2 tbsps. butter
1 small onion, finely chopped
2 garlic cloves, minced
1 pint clams, minced
½ cup dry white wine
2 tbsps. minced parsley
1 tbsp. olive oil
¼ tbsp. white pepper
1 cup flavored bread crumbs
12 cherrystone clam shells (scrubbed clean)

Heat oil and butter in a skillet. Add onion and garlic and sauté over medium heat until golden. Drain clam liquid into onion mixture, stir in wine, and simmer for about 5 minutes.

Mix in clams, parsley, olive oil, and pepper. Heat thoroughly. Spoon into clam shells and top with bread crumbs. Preheat oven to 375° F. Bake for about 15 minutes.

Cecil Kent
Ladder 156

SALMON MOUSSE

Servings: 20

2 envelopes unflavored gelatin
½ cup cold water
2 (15 oz.) cans pink salmon, drained (reserve
    liquid)
1 cup sour cream
1 cup mayonnaise
¼ cup lemon juice
1 tsp. salt, 1 tsp. paprika, 1 tsp. hot pepper
    sauce
Lettuce and lemon wedges for garnish

Soften gelatin in water, with salmon liquid added to total 1 cup. Stir over medium heat until gelatin dissolves. Cool. Place in a blender with remaining ingredients (except garnish) and blend till smooth. Pour into a lightly oiled 8-cup mold. Cover. Chill until set. Turn mold onto lettuce-lined plate; top with lemon wedges.

Joe Ginley
Engine 8, Retired

SHRIMP MOLD

Servings: 8–10

1 can tomato soup
3 small packages Philadelphia cream cheese
1½ packages unflavored gelatin
3 small cans (4½ oz.) deveined shrimp
1 cup mayonnaise
1 cup finely chopped celery
1 bunch scallions, stems only, chopped

Keep cream cheese out to soften. Heat soup over low heat and add cream cheese. Simmer till cheese is melted. Dissolve gelatin in ¼ cup cold water and add to tomato soup along with remaining ingredients. Stir. Pour into lightly greased mold. Chill overnight. Serve with crackers, potato chips, or pretzels.

Danny Rella
Engine 91

CRAB STUFFED MUSHROOMS

Servings: 12–15

3 dozen large fresh mushrooms
1 (7½ oz.) can crab meat, drained and flaked
1 tbsp. snipped parsley
1 tbsp. chopped pimiento
1 tsp. chopped capers
1 tsp. dry mustard
½ cup mayonnaise

Wash and dry mushrooms; remove stems. Combine crab meat, parsley, pimiento, capers, and chopped mushroom stems. Blend mustard and mayonnaise, toss with crab meat. Fill mushroom caps with mixture. Bake at 375° F for 10 minutes.

Joe Ginley
Engine 8, Retired

EGGPLANT, SPANISH STYLE

Servings: 8

2 medium eggplants, quartered and boiled
    until tender
8 eggs
8 ozs. cream cheese
8 ozs. farmer cheese
4 tbsps. grated Italian cheese
Salt and pepper to taste

Scoop out eggplant (save skins) and blend with remaining ingredients. Lightly grease a large roasting pan and line bottom with eggplant skins. Pour mixture over and dot with butter. Bake at 350° F for about 1 hour.

Nick Santimauro
Ladder 166

EGGPLANT ROLLUPS

Servings: 4

1 large eggplant, sliced lengthwise
2 eggs, beaten
Bread crumbs
Garlic, finely chopped
Ricotta cheese
Mozzarella, grated
Parsley, chopped
Marinara sauce

Dip eggplant slices in eggs, then in bread crumbs seasoned with garlic. Brown lightly; lay on a platter. Mix ricotta, mozzarella, and parsley. Spoon a heaping tablespoon onto each eggplant slice and roll, securing with toothpicks. Lay in a broiling pan and cover with marinara sauce. Bake at 450° F for 10–15 minutes.

John Sineno
Engine 58

ZUCCHINI APPETIZER

Servings: 8

3 cups shredded zucchini
1 cup Bisquick
½ cup chopped onion
½ cup grated Parmesan cheese
2 tbsps. chopped parsley
½ tsp. salt
1 tsp. Italian seasoning
½ tsp. oregano or marjoram
½ cup vegetable oil
Pepper to taste
4 eggs, beaten
1 garlic clove, chopped

Combine all ingredients in a bowl. Spread in a greased 13" x 9" pan. Preheat oven to 350° F and bake for 35 minutes until golden brown.

Mrs. Shirley Reed
Secretary to the Fire Commissioner

ZUCCHINI CASSEROLE

Servings: 14

6 lbs. fresh zucchini
3 (10 oz.) cans stewed tomatoes
1 lb. Swiss cheese, sliced
1¼ cups flavored bread crumbs

Cut zucchini into ½-inch slices. Parboil for approximately 7 minutes (zucchini is to remain firm). Drain thoroughly.

In a 13″ x 9″ pan, arrange a layer of zucchini, layer of stewed tomatoes, then a single layer of Swiss cheese. Repeat layers until zucchini is finished; end with a layer of cheese. Sprinkle with flavored bread crumbs. Bake at 375° F for 25 minutes.

Stephen "Whitefish" Ternlund
Ladder 108

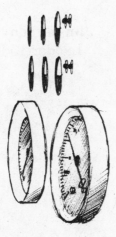

STUFFED ARTICHOKES

Servings: 6–8

6 medium artichokes
1 small onion, diced
2 garlic cloves, chopped
4 tbsps. oil
1½ cups flavored bread crumbs
¼ cup grated cheese
Salt and pepper

Cut stem and tops off each artichoke and wash. Pry open, and remove prickly choke. Sauté onion and garlic in 3 tablespoons oil. When tender, add bread crumbs, cheese, salt and pepper. Stuff each artichoke thoroughly and place in a pot, adding enough water to cover bottom half of artichokes; add 1 tablespoon oil. Simmer until tender, about 1 hour.

Jim Munday
Ladder 156

CURRIED BAKED CAULIFLOWER

Servings: 8–10

1 large cauliflower
½ tsp. salt
1 (10½ oz.) can condensed cream of
    chicken soup
1 cup grated Cheddar cheese
⅓ cup mayonnaise
1 tsp. curry powder
¼ cup dried bread crumbs
2 tbsps. butter or margarine, melted

Break cauliflower into flowerets. Steam about 10 minutes in 1 inch of water and salt in a large covered saucepan over medium-low heat. In a 2-quart casserole, combine undiluted soup, cheese, mayonnaise, and curry powder. Add cauliflower and mix well. Toss bread crumbs in melted butter or margarine and sprinkle on top. Bake 30 minutes at 350° F, until casserole is hot and bubbly.

John Sineno
Engine 58

FRIED CABBAGE

Servings: 6–8

1–2 lbs. cabbage
⅓ cup oil
6 garlic cloves, minced
Salt and pepper to taste

Remove any outer leaves of the cabbage that are dirty or bruised. Cut cabbage in half through the core. Rinse and drain thoroughly. Remove the core and discard. Slice cabbage lengthwise into half-inch strips. Set aside.

In a large skillet or wok, heat oil on medium to high heat and add garlic. (At this point you can add a couple of sliced onions if desired.) Sauté garlic till tender; do not let garlic brown. Add the cabbage and stir-fry until cabbage begins to soften. Add the salt and pepper and cook until cabbage is tender but not too soft, about 15 minutes. Do not brown cabbage. You can cook it more or less time according to the texture you like. Remove from heat and serve. It is delicious with any kind of pork or ham dish.

Carl J. Fargione
Engine 309

SCALLOPED POTATOES AND ONIONS

Servings: 4

5 large potatoes, peeled and sliced thin
¾ cup chopped onion
3 tbsps. butter or margarine
¼ cup all-purpose flour
1¾ cups chicken broth
1½ tbsps. mayonnaise
¾ tsp. salt
⅛ tsp. pepper
Paprika

In a round casserole dish, layer potatoes and onions alternately. In a saucepan, melt butter or margarine, blend in flour. Gradually stir in broth, mayonnaise, salt, and pepper. Cook, stirring frequently, until sauce bubbles and thickens. Pour over potatoes, sprinkle with paprika. Bake in a preheated 350° F oven for 1¼ hrs.

Capt. Joe Curry
Ladder 26

CANDIED SWEET POTATOES

Servings: 6

6 large sweet potatoes
¼ cup Kahlúa liqueur
Miniature marshmallows

Boil sweet potatoes. Mash and add liqueur. Pour into a baking dish and sprinkle with marshmallows. Bake in a 350° F oven till marshmallows are melted.

John Sineno
Engine 58

SCUNGILLI (CONCH) SALAD

Servings: 4–6

4 (8 oz.) cans scungilli
1 garlic clove, coarsely chopped
3 ozs. oil
3 ozs. lemon juice
1 tbsp. oregano
1 tbsp. basil flakes
1 tbsp. parsley flakes
Black pepper

Rinse scungilli with cold water. Put scungilli in a large jar. Add garlic, oil, lemon, oregano, basil, and parsley. Sprinkle with black pepper. Close jar tight; shake well. Put in refrigerator and shake occasionally. The longer it stays the sharper the taste. Serve *whenever*.

Squid salad is prepared in much the same way. Before adding to jar, boil 8 large squid in water for 2–3 minutes. Cut into bite-size pieces then proceed as above.

John Sineno
Engine 58

 COLESLAW

Servings: about 8–10 (depending upon size of cabbage)

1 large head cabbage
2 large carrots, shredded
1 large green pepper, chopped
Mayonnaise
2–3 tbsps. white vinegar
Salt
Pepper
½ tsp. sugar

Cut cabbage in half; core and shred. Mix cabbage, carrots, and pepper with mayonnaise. Add white vinegar and continue to blend. Add salt, pepper, and sugar. Stir. Refrigerate till well chilled, stirring occasionally.

David Vredenburgh
Engine 248

FRIED RICE

Servings: 6–8

1½ cups rice
3 cups water, lightly salted
10 strips bacon, cut into pieces
1 medium onion, diced
2 eggs, beaten
¼–½ cup soy sauce
½ tsp. garlic powder

Cook rice in the water. In a large frying pan, cook bacon until crisp. Remove. Cook onion in bacon grease; add eggs and stir. Add bacon and cooked rice to frying pan; add soy sauce. Flavor with garlic powder. Cook until rice is golden brown. Bean sprouts, mushrooms, and/or peas can be added for variety.

Jim Munday
Ladder 156

FIREHOUSE PANCAKES

Servings: 4–6

1⅓ cups milk
2 eggs, lightly beaten
8 tbsps. butter, melted
2 cups sifted flour
1 cup confectioner's sugar
4 tsps. baking powder
½ tsp. salt
Oil

Mix milk, eggs, and butter. Combine flour, sugar, baking powder, and salt. Stir milk mixture into flour mixture until moistened. Heat lightly oiled griddle until hot. Spoon mixture onto griddle and cook until bubbles appear evenly over top. Turn; cook second side until golden.

Nick Santimauro
Ladder 166

POTATO PANCAKES

Servings: 8–10

5 lbs. potatoes, peeled and shredded
4–5 large onions, chopped
Flour
Salt and pepper
½ tsp. baking powder
2 eggs

Combine potatoes, onions, flour, salt, pepper, and baking powder. Blend in beaten eggs. Add additional flour to create a mixture that's neither too stiff nor too loose. In a large black iron frying pan, heat cooking oil. With a large spoon, drop mixture into oil. Allow to brown and then flip. Rotate to cook evenly. Serve hot with applesauce, sour cream, or try ketchup and sweet relish.

David Vredenburgh
Engine 248

BETTY'S POTATO STUFFING

Servings: 12

6 lbs. potatoes
8 tbsps. butter or margarine
¼ cup milk
1 large onion
3 garlic cloves
1 lb. chopped meat
Salt and pepper, to taste
Garlic powder to taste
5 chestnuts, chopped, optional

Peel, quarter, and boil potatoes until tender, 20 to 30 minutes. Mash with 1 tablespoon butter and the milk. Chop and brown onions and garlic in 4 tablespoons butter. Add chopped meat and brown, breaking up meat into small pieces. Add meat to mashed potatoes. Season with salt, pepper, and garlic powder. Add chestnuts. Stuff uncooked turkey or chicken roast. Any mixture left over can be baked in a 350° F oven for 30 minutes.

POTATO BALLS

Servings: 8

6 large potatoes, cooked and mashed
2 eggs
¾ cup flour
½ cup plain bread crumbs
¼ tbsps. salt

Place cooled mashed potatoes in a covered bowl in refrigerator overnight. Put potatoes in bowl and add egg, flour, bread crumbs and salt. Mix well. Roll into balls about 1–1½ inches in diameter. Place in boiling water. When they rise to the top (about 3 minutes), remove and serve.

Joe Bryant
Rescue 3

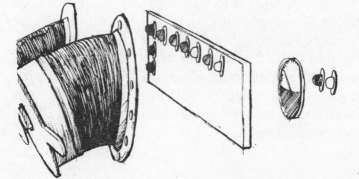

SAUSAGE BREAD

Servings: 16–20

Dough
2 cups flour
1 package yeast
2 tsps. salt
2 cups water
3 tbsps. oil
Filling
12–14 Italian sausages, remove meat from
    casing
1 small stick pepperoni, cut into small pieces
6–7 medium onions, chopped
Salt to taste

Mix all dough ingredients and knead.

Sauté onions in oil; when tender, add sausage, pepperoni, and salt. Sauté till sausage is thoroughly cooked.

Cut dough into 5 or 6 pieces. Roll out each piece of dough into 8″ x 12″ rectangles. Place filling over dough and roll; press ends together to seal roll. Place rolls, seam side down, on a greased baking pan. Cook in 375° F oven for 1 hour, until crust is golden brown. (You can baste each roll, while cooking, with juice from bottom of pan.)

John Sineno
Engine 58

BISHOP'S BREAD

Servings: 10–12

2⅔ cup flour (sifted)
3 tsps. baking powder
1 tsp. salt
1 cup brown sugar (firmly packed)
8 tbsps. butter or margarine
2 eggs
1 cup milk

Crumb Topping:
½ cup sugar
½ cup flour
4 tbsps. butter
1 tsp. cinnamon

Preheat oven to 375° F. Grease a 13″ x 9″ x 2″ baking pan. Sift together the flour, baking powder, and salt. In a large mixing bowl, blend brown sugar and butter. Add eggs and beat until the mixture is light and fluffy. Stir in milk. Add flour mixture and beat till all ingredients are combined. Turn the batter into the prepared pan.

For the topping, combine the sugar and flour with the butter and cinnamon to make crumbs. Sprinkle on top of batter. Bake for 25 minutes.

Mrs. Shirley Reed
Secretary to the Fire Commissioner

NAN'S IRISH SODA BREAD

Servings: 12 (2 loaves)

8 cups unbleached flour
1 box raisins
1 cup sugar
16 level tsps. baking powder
1 tsp. salt
2 sticks lightly salted butter
1 quart milk
3 large eggs

Preheat oven to 450° F. Blend flour, raisins, sugar, baking powder, and salt with a wooden spoon. Slowly melt butter in a separate pan and pour ½ quart milk and 3 beaten eggs into pan. Combine all ingredients and the remaining ½ quart milk until the batter is of a thick consistency. Pour batter into two bread pans, three-quarters full; use the remaining batter for muffin pans. Place pans in oven:

    * *20 minutes for muffins*
    * *1 hour for bread*

    Lower oven to 425° F after 10 minutes; then lower to 375° F after ½ hour.

Ron Darcy
Engine 276

DESSERTS

CHEESECAKE

Servings: 12–16

Filling:
3 lbs. cream cheese
7 eggs
1½ cups sugar
1 tbsp. vanilla
1 tbsp. lemon juice
1 tbsp. flour
1 cup half-and-half

Crust:
6 graham crackers
3 tbsp. butter

For the crust, mix crushed graham crackers and butter and pack firmly in bottom of a 10-inch springform pan.

For the filling, all ingredients should be at room temperature. Mix cream cheese and eggs together, one at a time, till smooth. Add sugar, vanilla, lemon juice, and flour. Gently fold in the half-and-half. Pour over graham crackers. Cook at 350° F for 1 hour. Leave in oven for another hour until cake cools. Refrigerate for at least 6 hours before serving.

Serve plain or with some blueberry, strawberry, or cherry preserves, or with chopped walnuts. For chocolate fiends: add 1½ cups mini chocolate chips to filling before cooking.

Frank Bernard
Ladder 26, Batt. 25

ITALIAN CHEESECAKE

Servings: 12–16

32 ozs. cream cheese
5–6 eggs
1½ cups sugar
2 tbsps. cornstarch
4 ozs. butter, melted
1 tsp. vanilla
1 tbsp. anise extract
1 tsp. coconut extract
1 tsp. brandy extract
1 tsp. orange extract
1 tsp. rum extract
1 tsp. lemon juice
16 ozs. ricotta cheese
2–3 ozs. citron dried fruit

Mix all ingredients except citron. When batter is well mixed, pour into a blender; add citron and blend thoroughly. Pour into a 10″ or 11″ springform pan. Place in a roasting pan half full of water. Bake in a 450° F oven for 1 hour. Let stand for 2 hours, then refrigerate for 3–6 hours before serving.

John Sineno
Engine 58

AMARETTO CHEESECAKE

Servings: 12–16

32 ozs. cream cheese
5–6 eggs
1½ cups sugar
2 tbsps. cornstarch
4 ozs. butter, melted
1 tbsp. vanilla
1 tbsp. lemon juice
16 ozs. sour cream
1 tbsp. almond extract
1 tbsp. orange extract
2 ozs. Amaretto liqueur

Crust:
2½ cups crushed coconut crackers
⅔ cup butter, melted

For the filling, mix all ingredients and set aside. Combine crust ingredients and blend thoroughly. Place this crust in a greased 9-inch springform pan. Pour in cheese mixture and sprinkle some crumbs from crust on top of batter before placing in oven. Place the springform pan in a roasting pan half full of water. Bake at 450° F for 1 hour. After cake is done, let set for 2 hours. Reverse cheesecake, so that the bottom becomes the top.

John Sineno
Engine 58

I was sitting in the firehouse kitchen thinking of what meal to cook for the next tour. I asked the men what they would like. John Glynn popped up, "You've been experimenting with different cheesecakes on other tours, how about making one for us?" So I made a pineapple cheesecake for the brothers that day. John Glynn said, "This is it! What do you want to call it?" I said, "We'll call it XC-4." Experimental Cheesecake Number 4. Everytime we had a "winner" we gave it a new number. We are now up to XC-24. This is a Piña Colada Cheesecake.

PIÑA COLADA CHEESECAKE

Servings: 12–16

32 ozs. cream cheese
5–6 eggs
1½ cups sugar
2 tbsps. cornstarch
4 ozs. butter, melted
1 tbsp. vanilla
1 tbsp. lemon juice
16 ozs. sour cream
1 tsp. rum flavor
1 cup coconut flakes
1 medium can of pineapple (tidbits or crushed)

In a bowl, combine all ingredients except coconut and pineapple, mixing thoroughly with a hand beater. Pour into a blender and add coconut. Blend well. Grease a 9-inch springform pan. Pour mixture from blender into pan. Drain off pineapple and layer on top. Place springform pan in a roasting pan half full with water. Bake at 450° F for 1 hour. After cake is done, let set for 3–4 hours.

John Sineno
Engine 58

APPLE CAKE

Servings: 8–10

3 cups flour
2 cups sugar
1 tsp. baking soda
1 tsp. cinnamon
1 tsp. salt
3 cups apples, diced
2 eggs
1 cup oil
1 tsp. vanilla
2 cups chopped nuts

Mix flour, sugar, soda, cinnamon, and salt with an electric mixer or food processor. Transfer to a large bowl. Make a well in the dry ingredients. Add the apples, eggs, oil, and vanilla. Stir by hand until mixed well. Add chopped nuts. Bake at 350° F for 45 minutes in a large square or oblong pan. Serve warm.

Capt. Joe Curry
Ladder 26

APPLE TART

Servings: 4

6 McIntosh apples
10″ pie crust
2 eggs
¼ cup sugar
½ cup heavy cream
½ cup milk

Preheat oven to 350° F. Cut each apple into 8 pieces and place in pie crust. Cook in oven for 20 minutes. Meanwhile, mix remaining ingredients. Pour over apples and cook an additional 20 minutes.

Joe Bryant
Rescue 3

TOP-ME-TWICE CAKE

Servings: 10

2 cups all-purpose flour
1 cup sugar
1 tsp. baking soda
1 tsp. salt
1 (13 oz.) can crushed pineapple
1 teaspoon vanilla
2 eggs

Blend and mix all cake ingredients for 2 minutes at low speed. Place in a 9-inch square, greased pan and cook at 350° F for 45 minutes.

Topping:
½ cup firm brown sugar
½ cup flaked coconut
½ cup chopped pecans

Sauce:
½ cup margarine
½ cup light cream
½ cup sugar
½ tsp. vanilla

When cake is done, remove from oven and pour topping and then sauce over cake. Return to oven and cook for an additional 10 minutes. Cool and serve.

Eugene Walsh, Jr.
Engine 54

LAZY DAISY CAKE

Servings: 8

2 eggs
1 cup sugar
1 tsp. vanilla
1 cup flour
2 tsps. baking soda
½ cup scalded milk
1 tbsp. butter

Beat eggs and add sugar and vanilla. Mix until light and fluffy. Add remaining ingredients one by one and continue to mix. Pour into a 9″ x 12″ greased pan and bake in a 375° F oven for 20 minutes.

Topping:
6 tbsps. butter
4 tbsps. evaporated milk or heavy cream
9 heaping tbsps. brown sugar
1 can shredded coconut

Melt butter, add milk and sugar, and blend. Fold in shredded coconut. Spread on cake while still hot. Return to oven and cook for an additional 3–5 minutes.

Chief Fred Gerken
Valiant Hose Co. #1
Bellrose, N.Y.

SOUR CREAM COFFEE CAKE

Servings 12–14

1 cup butter or margarine, softened
2 cups sugar
1 pint sour cream
2 tsps. baking soda
4 eggs
2 tsps. vanilla
3 cups sifted flour
3 tsps. baking powder

Topping:
½ cup sugar
2 tsps. cinnamon
½ cup chopped nuts
2 tsps. unsweetened cocoa (more, if desired)

Cream butter and sugar. Add sour cream and baking soda. Add eggs, one at a time, beating well. Add vanilla, flour, and baking powder. Mix well. Pour into a greased and floured pan 14½" x 10" x 2", or into two 8-inch square pans. Mix topping ingredients and sprinkle half this mixture over batter; run knife through to marbleize. Sprinkle remaining topping over blended batter. Cook in a 350° F oven for 45 minutes.

Chuck Zuba
Ladder 26

PUMPKIN PIE

Servings: 8

1 cup firmly packed brown sugar
1 tbsp. flour
1 tbsp. pumpkin pie spice (or 1¼ tsps.
    cinnamon, ½ tsp. nutmeg, and ½ tsp.
    ginger)
½ tsp. salt
1 (1 lb.) can pumpkin, or 2 cups fresh-cooked
    pumpkin, puréed
1 slightly beaten egg
1 (12 oz.) can evaporated milk
Unbaked deep-dish pastry crust

Mix in a large bowl brown sugar, flour, pumpkin spices, and salt. Add pumpkin and blend till smooth. Stir in egg and milk. Pour into 9-inch unbaked crust. Bake in a 375° F oven for 55–60 minutes, or until knife inserted 2 inches from edge comes out clean.

Chuck Zuba
Ladder 26

PECAN PIE

Servings: 8

1 cup sugar
4 tbsps. melted butter
4 eggs
2 tbsps. dark rum
1 tbsp. vanilla
¾ cup light corn syrup
½ cup dark corn syrup
½ lb. pecans, halved
1 frozen pie crust

Preheat oven to 350° F. Blend sugar and butter. Add eggs, rum, vanilla, and corn syrups. Pour pecans into pie crust until three-quarters full. Pour syrup mixture over. Bake for about 50 minutes, or until golden brown.

Carol B. Hafer
Counsel to F.D.N.Y.

Engine 91 often responds to the same alarms as Engine 58. One morning, as both companies were repacking their hoses after a small tenement fire, one of the men from Engine 91 asked if I'd make them a tray of rice pudding that they might have with their lunch. I said I'd be glad to and would start on it as soon as I got back to quarters.

Knowing my guys I knew they'd also want rice pudding if I made a tray for 91 Engine, so I decided to make two trays of pudding instead of one.

When the cooking was done I left both trays of pudding on the kitchen table to cool and went upstairs to wash up. Ed Fealey couldn't resist the temptation to pull a gag. While I was upstairs Fealey put some spoons, forks, and knives into one of the trays of pudding where they naturally sank to the bottom.

When I returned to the kitchen I topped off the pudding with cinnamon and called Engine 91 to tell them that they could pick up their pudding whenever they were ready.

Shortly thereafter we received another alarm to which Engine 91 also responded. They were dismissed from the scene before we were so they decided to stop by our firehouse on the way back to theirs and pick up their tray of pudding.

A few days later we caught another job along with Engine 91. After the fire had been extinguished and we were "taking up," I asked one of the guys from Engine 91 if they had enjoyed the pudding. "John, it was great. But how did you know that we needed silverware?" one of the guys replied. I didn't know what he was talking about and thought about it all the way back to quarters. It wasn't until we got back and were having a cup of coffee in the kitchen that Ed Fealey could no longer restrain his mirth and blurted out his silverware caper. He professed complete innocence, however, in extending the gag to include the guys at 91.

"I played the joke on our guys. How was I to know it would ricochet," he said.

OLE FASHIONED CREAMY RICE PUDDING

Servings: 8–10

1 quart whole milk
¼ tsp. salt
1 cup white rice (rinsed in cold water and
      drained)
2 eggs
1 cup evaporated milk
1 tsp. vanilla
½ cup sugar
½ cup raisins (parboiled for 15 minutes)

Place whole milk and salt into a saucepan. When milk is warm, add rice. Bring to a slow boil and then reduce to a simmer, stirring continually. Cook till rice is soft, about 45 minutes.

Meanwhile, in a large bowl, blend the eggs, ¾ cup of evaporated milk, vanilla, and sugar. Set aside.

Add ¼ cup evaporated milk to rice. Stir. Add raisins. The mixture should be thickening. When rice is soft, spoon 1 cup of rice mixture into blended eggs, stir, and then slowly pour egg mixture into remaining rice and cook until it becomes bubbly and thick. Pour into a bowl and sprinkle with nutmeg. Serve warm or cold.

David Vredenburgh
Engine 248

HOLIDAY ITALIAN FIG COOKIES

Servings: 10 cookies

2 (8 oz.) packages figs on string
2 (8 oz.) packages dates
1 (8 oz.) can slivered almonds
1 lb. honey
1 cup water
Black pepper
4 boxes Flako Pie crust

Chop figs and dates and add almonds. Combine honey and water and cook about ½ hour until soft. Add dates, figs, almonds, and black pepper to honey. Let cool. Prepare dough and roll into 5" x 10" rectangles. Spoon fruit and honey mixture onto half of each rectangle. Fold dough over mixture. Cut diagonally. Bake in a 375° F oven for 10 minutes. Cool. (The older the better, cookies will last about 1 month.)

John Sineno
Engine 58

Rum Balls

Servings: 2 dozen

2½ cups vanilla wafer crumbs (about ½ lb.)
1 cup pecans, chopped
2 tbsps. cocoa
¼ cup light corn syrup
¼ cup rum
Confectioners' sugar

Mix vanilla wafers and chopped nuts. Add cocoa, syrup, and rum; mix well. Coat hands with confectioners' sugar and roll mixture into balls ½ to ¾ inch in diameter. Refrigerate for about 1 hour; roll in confectioners' sugar and serve.

Joe Pinto
Engine 58

One day Danny Prince, Ladder 156, called me and said, "John, I need a few recipes to include in a cookbook. It's a fundraiser for Father Brady." I said I'd be glad to help. I'd even bake a few cakes for the event. Gerard O'Donnell, executive assistant to the fire commissioner, came up to me a few days later and asked to have his name on one of the cakes I was baking for the church fundraiser. I told him that would be no problem.

On a pistachio chocolate chip mousse I put the initials G.O.D. Several weeks after the event I met Danny and asked if everything went all right. He assured me that the fundraiser was a big success but then drew me aside and asked: "Was the mousse marked GOD intended as some special gesture for Father Brady?"

When I stopped laughing, I told him it was the abbreviation for *Gerard O'D*onnell.

PISTACHIO MOUSSE

Servings: 4–6

2 packages pistachio pudding and pie filling
18 ozs. whipped cream or Cool Whip
1 cup milk
Handful of chocolate chips

Mix all ingredients together and refrigerate.
You can use any of the following instant pudding flavors: chocolate chip
                chocolate mint
                butter almond
                vanilla
                toasted coconut
                banana cream

John Sineno
Engine 58

HONEY BUTTER BRITTLE

Servings: 10

1 cup toasted walnuts, coarsely chopped
1 cup butter
½ cup brown sugar, firmly packed
½ cup honey
Dash of salt
1 tsp. vanilla

To toast walnuts, spread on a cookie sheet and heat in a 350° F oven for 10 minutes, stirring frequently. In a large saucepan, combine butter, brown sugar, honey, and salt. Bring to a boil, stirring. Add ½ cup nuts. Continue cooking on *low*, stirring frequently to hard crack stage* (300° F on a candy thermometer; rushing this procedure will only cause mixture to burn). Add vanilla. Pour candy into a well-buttered 8-inch square cake pan. Cover top with remaining walnuts and press into candy. When candy is cold, turn out of pan and break into small irregular pieces.

Fireman 1st. Grade Warren G. Kessler
Engine 268

* If no thermometer is available, put cold water in a glass and drop a small amount of mixture into water. If candy forms a hard ball, candy is done.

RECIPE FOR A FIREFIGHTER

IN MEMORY OF
CAPTAIN JAMES F. MCDONNELL

INGREDIENTS:

Strength	Wisdom
Humility	Courage
Endurance	Patience
Humor	Glaze of Love

NOTE: Firefighters are prepared and blended only over many years.

Set aside a small child.

Sprinkle generously with active play to mold a strong body.

Add liberally, stirring slowly, huge handfuls of humor—a firefighter will not gel without it.

Watch carefully for approximately 13 years until the child turns into a spirited youth.

Add the seeds of wisdom that only grow through youthful trial and error.

Knead continuously through the teen years until endurance is blended with strength.

Add slowly the yeast of humility.

Set aside for 3 or 4 years allowing the dough time to rise and double.

Call in master chefs with the recipe engraved upon their hearts for the final work.

Punch down the fully risen dough to shape the loaf.

Roll carefully using the rolling pin of training on the well-floured board of discipline.

Blend in the rare spice of courage found hidden between the leaves of foolishness and cowardice that is only purchased with the gold of sacrifice.

Shape the loaf with care, and brush with the glaze of love to make them shine.

It is this glaze of love for human life that makes them what they are. The love that makes them stand and risk life, health and security for strangers until their job is done, and they hear these precious words:

"Well done—good and faithful servant."

Betty Lines
December, 1985